CYSTIC FIBROSIS HEALTHCARE EDUCATION

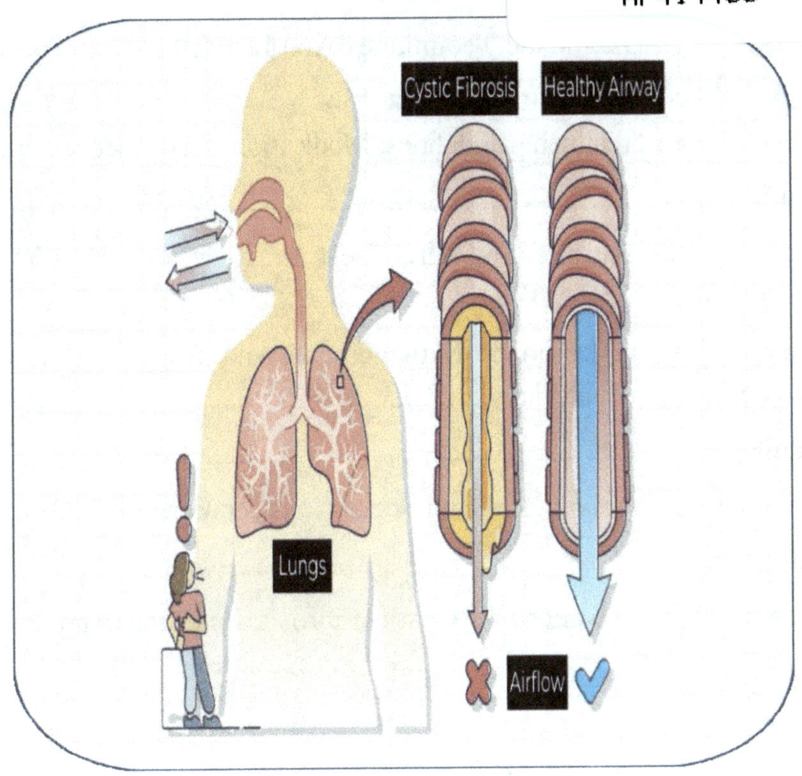

TABLE OF CONTENTS

COURSE OVERVIEW

This course provides an in-depth exploration of cystic fibrosis (CF), aimed at equipping healthcare professionals with the knowledge and skills necessary to deliver exceptional care to patients with CF. The course is designed for respiratory therapists, doctors, nurses, dietitians, psychologists, and other healthcare providers who play a vital role in the management of cystic fibrosis. Through a combination of lectures, case studies, and interactive discussions, participants will gain a thorough understanding of best practices in CF care and learn to apply this knowledge in clinical settings.

COURSE OBJECTIVES

The objectives of this course is to let participants Understand the Genetic and Pathophysiological Basis of CF, Identify and Manage Clinical Signs and Symptoms, Utilize Diagnostic Imaging and Testing Effectively, Implement Comprehensive Treatment Plans, Optimize Respiratory and Nutritional Care, Address Psychological and Social Aspects of CF, Stay Informed on Advances in CF Research, Apply Knowledge Through Case Studies, By the end of this course, participants will have a comprehensive understanding of cystic fibrosis and be equipped with the tools necessary to provide high-quality, informed, and compassionate care to individuals living with CF.

COURSE MATERIALS

To learn this course, **healthcare providers/ participants** must be provided with materials like a Pen, pencil, notebook, and notepad to better understand and make it easy for them to learn.

INTRODUCTION

Cystic fibrosis (CF) is a complex and challenging disease that affects thousands of individuals worldwide. This inherited disorder primarily impacts the respiratory and digestive systems, leading to severe chronic respiratory infections and pancreatic enzyme insufficiency. As a healthcare provider, understanding the intricacies of CF is crucial in delivering high-quality care and improving patient outcomes.

Mastering Cystic Fibrosis Care: A Comprehensive Guide for Healthcare Providers" is designed to serve as an all-encompassing resource for respiratory therapists, doctors, nurses, and other healthcare professionals who are dedicated to the treatment and management of CF. This book provides an in-depth look at every aspect of the disease, from the basics of its pathophysiology to the latest advancements in treatment and care.

Through this comprehensive guide, we aim to equip healthcare providers with the knowledge and tools necessary to deliver exceptional care to individuals with cystic fibrosis. By understanding the disease in its entirety, from pathophysiology to treatment and beyond, providers can make a significant impact on the lives of their patients.

<h1 style="text-align:center"><u>MODULE ONE</u></h1>

<h2 style="text-align:center"><u>LESSON ONE: CYSTIC FIBROSIS</u></h2>

Cystic fibrosis (CF) is one of the most common life-threatening genetic disorders, affecting approximately 70,000 people worldwide. It is an autosomal recessive disorder caused by mutations in the cystic fibrosis transmembrane conductance regulator (CFTR) gene. The CFTR gene is responsible for encoding a protein that regulates the movement of salt and water in and out of cells. Mutations in this gene lead to the production of a defective CFTR protein, resulting in the accumulation of thick, sticky mucus in various organs, primarily the lungs and digestive system.

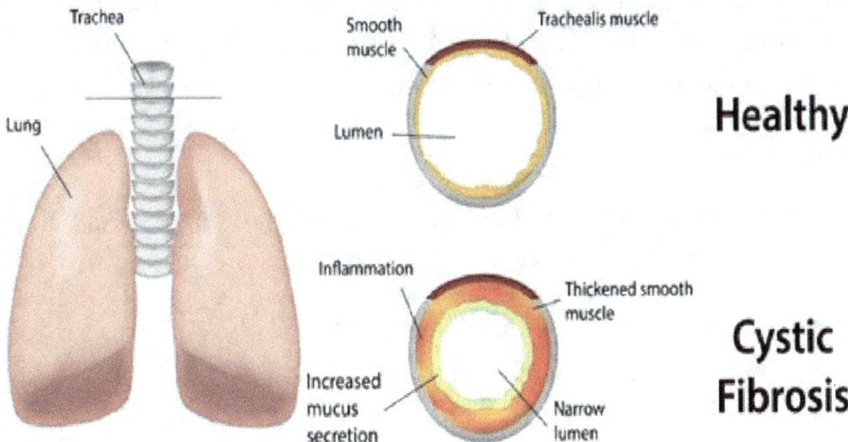

Genetic Basis and Epidemiology

CF is inherited in an autosomal recessive pattern, meaning that an individual must inherit two defective copies of the CFTR gene, one from each parent, to develop the disease. Carriers, who have only one defective copy, typically do not show symptoms but can pass the gene to their offspring. The most common mutation, ΔF508, accounts for approximately 70% of all CF cases, though over 2,000 different mutations have been identified.

CF primarily affects Caucasians of Northern European descent, with an incidence of about 1 in 2,500 to 3,500 newborns. However, it is present in all ethnic groups. Advances in newborn screening and genetic testing have improved early diagnosis, allowing for timely intervention and better management of the disease.

Pathophysiology

The defective CFTR protein in CF patients leads to the production of abnormally thick and sticky mucus. This mucus obstructs the airways and ducts in various organs, causing the characteristic symptoms of the disease. In the lungs, mucus buildup leads to chronic infections and inflammation, resulting in progressive lung damage. In the digestive system, thick mucus blocks the ducts of the pancreas, preventing digestive enzymes from reaching the intestines and leading to malabsorption of nutrients.

Clinical Features

The clinical presentation of CF can vary widely among patients. Some of the common signs and symptoms include:

- Persistent cough with thick mucus
- Frequent lung infections
- Wheezing and shortness of breath
- Poor growth and weight gain despite a good appetite
- Greasy, bulky stools
- Male infertility
- Diagnosis

Early diagnosis of CF is crucial for initiating appropriate treatments and improving outcomes. Newborn screening programs typically include a test for immunoreactive trypsinogen (IRT), a pancreatic enzyme precursor that is elevated in CF. Positive screening results are followed by confirmatory tests, such as sweat chloride tests and genetic testing, to identify CFTR mutations.

Treatment

While there is no cure for CF, various treatments aim to manage symptoms, prevent complications, and improve quality of life. Treatment plans are individualized based on the severity of the disease and the organs affected. Key components of CF management include:

- Airway clearance techniques to remove mucus from the lungs
- Inhaled medications to open airways and thin mucus
- Antibiotics to treat lung infections
- Pancreatic enzyme supplements to aid digestion
- Nutritional support to maintain a healthy weight
- Multidisciplinary Care

CF care requires a multidisciplinary approach involving a team of healthcare providers, including pulmonologists, gastroenterologists, dietitians, respiratory therapists, and nurses. This team collaborates to address the various aspects of the disease and provide comprehensive care tailored to each patient's needs.

Advances in CF Research

Ongoing research is continually improving our understanding of CF and leading to the development of new treatments. CFTR modulators, which target the underlying cause of CF by improving the function of the defective CFTR protein, have revolutionized CF care for many patients. Clinical trials and research into gene therapy and other innovative treatments offer hope for further advancements and improved outcomes for individuals with CF.

DISCUSSION QUESTIONS

- How does the genetic mutation in the CFTR gene lead to the characteristic symptoms of cystic fibrosis?
- What are the current challenges in diagnosing cystic fibrosis in different age groups, and how can they be addressed?

LESSON TWO: CLINICAL PRESENTATION AND PHYSIOLOGICAL SIGNS

Cystic fibrosis (CF) presents a wide range of clinical manifestations that can vary significantly from one patient to another. Recognizing these signs and symptoms early is crucial for diagnosis and intervention, which can ultimately improve patient outcomes. This lesson delves into the clinical presentation and physiological signs of CF, providing healthcare providers with the knowledge needed to identify and manage this multifaceted disease.

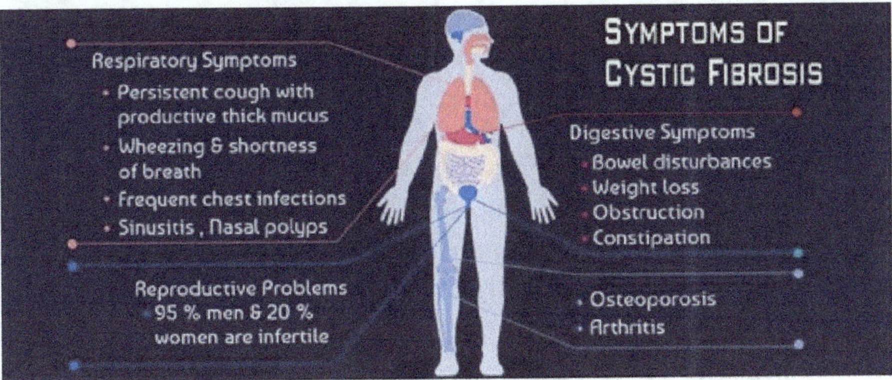

Respiratory System

The respiratory system is the primary organ system affected by CF. The thick, sticky mucus characteristic of the disease obstructs the airways, leading to recurrent respiratory infections and chronic inflammation. Common respiratory symptoms include:

- Chronic Cough: Persistent coughing, often accompanied by thick, purulent sputum, is a hallmark of CF. This cough may be present from early childhood and can worsen over time.
- Wheezing and Shortness of Breath: Airway obstruction can cause wheezing and difficulty breathing, particularly during physical activity or respiratory infections.

- Frequent Lung Infections: Patients with CF are prone to lung infections caused by bacteria such as Pseudomonas aeruginosa and Staphylococcus aureus. These infections can lead to increased coughing, sputum production, and fever.
- Nasal Polyps and Sinusitis: Chronic inflammation in the sinuses can result in nasal polyps and recurrent sinus infections, contributing to breathing difficulties and a decreased sense of smell.

Digestive System

The digestive system is also significantly impacted by CF due to the blockage of pancreatic ducts by thick mucus, preventing digestive enzymes from reaching the intestines. This leads to malabsorption and various gastrointestinal symptoms:

- Poor Growth and Weight Gain: Despite having a normal or increased appetite, children with CF may experience poor growth and weight gain due to malabsorption of nutrients.
- Steatorrhea: Fatty, bulky, and foul-smelling stools are a common symptom resulting from the inability to digest fats properly.
- Meconium Ileus: In newborns, a thick, sticky first stool (meconium) can cause intestinal blockage, known as meconium ileus. This condition is often the first indication of CF.
- Abdominal Pain and Distension: Blockages in the intestines can cause abdominal pain, bloating, and discomfort.

Endocrine System

CF can affect the endocrine system, leading to complications such as:

- Cystic Fibrosis-Related Diabetes (CFRD): The thick mucus can damage the pancreas over time, affecting its ability to produce insulin and leading to diabetes.

- Delayed Puberty: Nutritional deficiencies and chronic illness can delay the onset of puberty in adolescents with CF.

Reproductive System

CF can impact reproductive health, particularly in males:

- Male Infertility: More than 95% of males with CF are infertile due to congenital bilateral absence of the vas deferens (CBAVD), which obstructs the transport of sperm.
- Female Fertility: While women with CF are generally fertile, thick cervical mucus can make it more difficult to conceive.

Musculoskeletal System

The musculoskeletal system can also be affected by CF, leading to:

- Arthritis and Osteoporosis: Chronic inflammation and nutritional deficiencies can contribute to joint pain and an increased risk of osteoporosis.

Psychological and Social Impact

The chronic nature of CF and its impact on daily life can have significant psychological and social effects on patients and their families:

- Anxiety and Depression: The stress of managing a chronic illness can lead to anxiety and depression in both patients and caregivers.
- Social Isolation: Frequent hospitalizations and the need to avoid infections can limit social interactions and participation in activities.

Recognizing Exacerbations

It is essential for healthcare providers to recognize the signs of CF exacerbations, which are periods of worsening symptoms often triggered by infections. These exacerbations may include:

- Increased cough and sputum production
- Changes in sputum color and consistency
- Fever
- Weight loss
- Decreased lung function
- Multisystem Involvement

CF is a multisystem disease, meaning that it can affect multiple organs and systems simultaneously. Healthcare providers must adopt a holistic approach to patient care, considering the interconnected nature of CF symptoms and their impact on overall health.

The clinical presentation and physiological signs of cystic fibrosis are diverse and can affect various organ systems. Early recognition and intervention are crucial in managing the disease and improving patient outcomes. By understanding the wide range of symptoms associated with CF, healthcare providers can better diagnose, treat, and support patients in their journey with this complex condition.

DISCUSSION QUESTIONS

- How do the respiratory and digestive symptoms of cystic fibrosis typically progress over a patient's lifetime?
- What are the most effective methods for monitoring and managing the progression of cystic fibrosis symptoms in children versus adults?

MODULE TWO

LESSON ONE: DIAGNOSTIC TECHNIQUES AND IMAGING; WHAT TO LOOK FOR IN X-RAYS

Early and accurate diagnosis of cystic fibrosis (CF) is vital for initiating appropriate treatments and improving patient outcomes. This lesson provides an in-depth look at the various diagnostic techniques used to confirm CF and the critical role of imaging studies, particularly chest X-rays, in assessing the extent of pulmonary involvement.

Posterior-Anterior CXR: Cystic Fibrosis

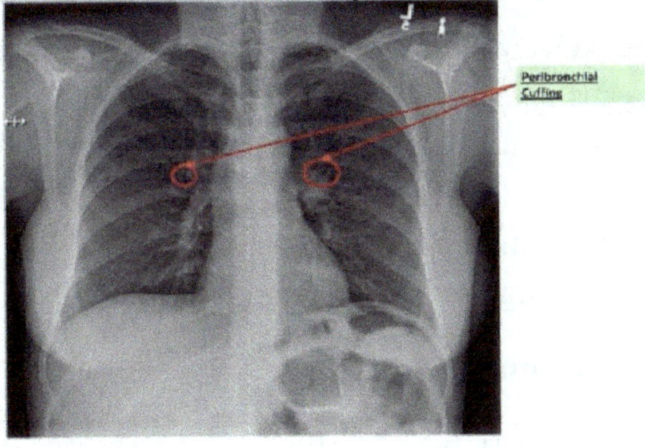

Newborn Screening

Newborn screening for CF has become a standard practice in many countries, allowing for early detection and intervention. The primary screening test used is the immunoreactive trypsinogen (IRT) test:

- Immunoreactive Trypsinogen (IRT) Test: This blood test measures the levels of trypsinogen, an enzyme precursor produced by the pancreas. Elevated IRT levels can indicate CF and warrant further testing.

11

Sweat Chloride Test

The sweat chloride test is the gold standard for diagnosing CF. It measures the concentration of chloride in the sweat, which is elevated in individuals with CF:

- Procedure: Pilocarpine iontophoresis is used to stimulate sweat production. Sweat is then collected and analyzed for chloride concentration.
- Diagnostic Criteria: A sweat chloride concentration of 60 mmol/L or higher is indicative of CF. Intermediate levels (30-59 mmol/L) may require further genetic testing.

Genetic Testing

Genetic testing is used to confirm the diagnosis of CF by identifying mutations in the CFTR gene:

- CFTR Mutation Analysis: This test detects common CF-causing mutations, including ΔF508. Comprehensive panels can identify a broader range of mutations.
- Carrier Testing: Genetic testing can also identify carriers of CF mutations, which is useful for family planning and assessing the risk of having a child with CF.

Pulmonary Function Tests (PFTs)

Pulmonary function tests (PFTs) are essential for assessing lung function in CF patients:

- Spirometry: This test measures the volume and flow of air during inhalation and exhalation. Key parameters include forced vital capacity (FVC) and forced expiratory volume in one second (FEV1).
- Lung Volumes and Diffusion Capacity: Additional PFTs can measure lung volumes and the ability of the lungs to transfer

gases, providing a comprehensive assessment of respiratory function.

Imaging Studies

Imaging studies, particularly chest X-rays, play a critical role in diagnosing and monitoring CF:

- Chest X-rays: Chest X-rays are commonly used to assess the extent of lung disease in CF. Key findings may include:
- Hyperinflation: Increased lung volumes due to air trapping.
- Bronchiectasis: Dilation and thickening of the bronchial walls.
- Mucus Plugs: Opacities representing mucus-filled airways.
- Atelectasis: Areas of collapsed lung tissue.
- High-Resolution Computed Tomography (HRCT): HRCT scans provide detailed images of the lungs and can detect early structural changes not visible on standard X-rays. HRCT is particularly useful for evaluating bronchiectasis and small airway disease.

Additional Diagnostic Tests

Other diagnostic tests may be used to assess the impact of CF on different organ systems:

- Stool Tests: Fecal elastase testing measures pancreatic enzyme production and can indicate pancreatic insufficiency.
- Liver Function Tests: Blood tests can assess liver function and detect liver disease, which is a potential complication of CF.
- Glucose Tolerance Test: This test evaluates glucose metabolism and can diagnose cystic fibrosis-related diabetes (CFRD).

Recognizing Radiographic Signs

Healthcare providers must be adept at recognizing radiographic signs of CF on chest X-rays:

- Mucus Plugging: Appears as linear or branching opacities.
- Bronchial Wall Thickening: Visible as parallel lines or "tram-tracks."
- Cystic Changes: Air-filled cysts or bullae resulting from bronchiectasis.
- Increased Lung Markings: Reflect chronic inflammation and infection.

Role of Imaging in Monitoring Disease Progression

Regular imaging studies are crucial for monitoring disease progression and guiding treatment decisions:

- Baseline and Follow-Up X-rays: Establishing a baseline chest X-ray at diagnosis allows for comparison with follow-up images to assess changes over time.
- Detecting Complications: Imaging can identify complications such as pneumothorax (collapsed lung), hemoptysis (coughing up blood), and chronic lung infections.

Integrating Diagnostic Information

A comprehensive diagnosis of CF involves integrating information from various diagnostic tests and clinical findings:

- Multidisciplinary Approach: Collaboration among pulmonologists, geneticists, radiologists, and other specialists ensures accurate diagnosis and effective management.
- Patient and Family Education: Educating patients and families about the diagnostic process and its implications is essential for fostering understanding and adherence to treatment plans.

Diagnosing cystic fibrosis requires a combination of clinical evaluation, genetic testing, and imaging studies. By understanding the diagnostic techniques and recognizing key radiographic signs, healthcare providers can accurately diagnose CF and monitor disease progression, ultimately improving patient outcomes.

DISCUSSION QUESTIONS

- What role does genetic testing play in the diagnosis and management of cystic fibrosis, and how can it be integrated with other diagnostic methods?
- How can advances in imaging techniques improve the early detection and monitoring of cystic fibrosis complications?

LESSON TWO: TREATMENT MODALITIES; MEDICATIONS AND THERAPIES

Effective management of cystic fibrosis (CF) involves a multifaceted approach that includes medications, therapies, and lifestyle modifications. This lesson provides a comprehensive overview of the treatment modalities available for CF, focusing on medications and therapeutic interventions that improve patient outcomes and quality of life.

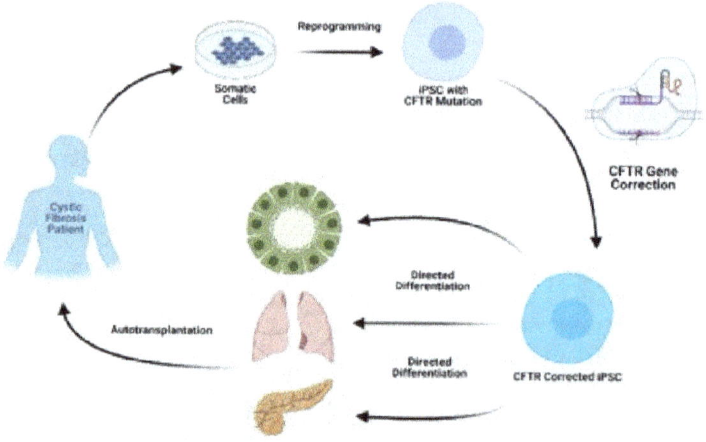

MEDICATIONS

A variety of medications are used to manage the symptoms and complications of CF. These include:

1. Mucolytics

Mucolytics are medications that help thin and loosen mucus in the airways, making it easier to cough up:

- Dornase Alfa (Pulmozyme): An enzyme that breaks down DNA in mucus, reducing its viscosity. It is administered via nebulization.
- Hypertonic Saline: Inhaled hypertonic saline solution draws water into the airways, thinning the mucus and facilitating its clearance.

2. Antibiotics

Antibiotics are crucial for treating and preventing lung infections in CF patients:

- Inhaled Antibiotics: Tobramycin and aztreonam are commonly used inhaled antibiotics that target Pseudomonas aeruginosa, a frequent cause of lung infections in CF.
- Oral and Intravenous Antibiotics: Depending on the severity of the infection, oral or intravenous antibiotics such as ciprofloxacin, ceftazidime, and meropenem may be prescribed.

3. CFTR Modulators

CFTR modulators are a class of medications that target the underlying cause of CF by improving the function of the defective CFTR protein:

- Ivacaftor (Kalydeco): A potentiator that enhances the activity of the CFTR protein at the cell surface, effective for certain CFTR mutations.
- Lumacaftor/Ivacaftor (Orkambi): A combination therapy that improves CFTR protein processing and function, used for patients with the ΔF508 mutation.
- Tezacaftor/Ivacaftor (Symdeko) and Elexacaftor/Tezacaftor/Ivacaftor (Trikafta): Combination therapies that target multiple aspects of CFTR protein function, effective for a broader range of mutations.

4. Anti-inflammatory Medications

Chronic inflammation is a hallmark of CF lung disease, and anti-inflammatory medications can help reduce this inflammation:

- Ibuprofen: High-dose ibuprofen has been shown to slow the decline in lung function in some CF patients.
- Corticosteroids: Oral and inhaled corticosteroids may be used to reduce airway inflammation, though their long-term use is limited due to potential side effects.

Bronchodilators

Bronchodilators help open the airways and improve airflow, making it easier to breathe:

- Short-Acting Beta-Agonists (SABAs): Albuterol and levalbuterol are commonly used SABAs that provide quick relief of bronchoconstriction.
- Long-Acting Beta-Agonists (LABAs): Salmeterol and formoterol are LABAs used for maintenance therapy to control symptoms.

AIRWAY CLEARANCE TECHNIQUES

Airway clearance techniques (ACTs) are essential for removing mucus from the lungs and preventing infections. These techniques include:

1. **Chest Physiotherapy (CPT)**
   - CPT involves manual percussion and vibration of the chest to loosen mucus, followed by coughing or huffing to expel it.
2. **Positive Expiratory Pressure (PEP) Therapy**
   - PEP therapy uses a device that creates resistance during exhalation, helping to keep the airways open and move mucus towards the larger airways for clearance.

3. **High-Frequency Chest Wall Oscillation (HFCWO)**
   - HFCWO devices, such as the vest, generate high-frequency vibrations to loosen mucus and facilitate its clearance.

NUTRITIONAL SUPPORT

Maintaining adequate nutrition is vital for CF patients due to malabsorption and increased energy needs:

1. **Pancreatic Enzyme Replacement Therapy (PERT)**
   - PERT involves taking pancreatic enzyme supplements with meals to aid in the digestion and absorption of nutrients.
2. **Vitamin and Mineral Supplements**
   - CF patients often require supplements of fat-soluble vitamins (A, D, E, and K) and other nutrients to prevent deficiencies.
3. **High-Calorie Diet**
   - A high-calorie, high-protein diet is recommended to support growth, maintain a healthy weight, and meet increased energy demands.

RESPIRATORY THERAPIES

Various respiratory therapies are used to manage CF symptoms and maintain lung function:

1. **Inhaled Medications**
   - Inhaled medications, including bronchodilators, mucolytics, and antibiotics, are administered via nebulizers or metered-dose inhalers (MDIs) to target the lungs directly.
2. **Oxygen Therapy**
   - Oxygen therapy may be required for CF patients with advanced lung disease who experience low blood oxygen levels.

MANAGEMENT OF COMPLICATIONS

CF is a multisystem disease that can lead to various complications requiring targeted interventions:

1. Cystic Fibrosis-Related Diabetes (CFRD)

Managing CFRD involves monitoring blood glucose levels, administering insulin, and following a balanced diet.

2. Gastrointestinal Complications

Treatment of gastrointestinal complications includes PERT, dietary modifications, and medications to manage symptoms such as acid reflux and constipation.

MULTIDISCIPLINARY CARE

Effective CF management requires a multidisciplinary approach involving various healthcare providers:

1. CF Care Team

A typical CF care team includes pulmonologists, gastroenterologists, endocrinologists, dietitians, respiratory therapists, nurses, and social workers. This team collaborates to provide comprehensive care tailored to each patient's needs.

2. Patient and Family Education

Educating patients and their families about CF, its management, and the importance of adherence to treatment regimens is crucial for optimizing outcomes.

ADVANCES IN CF TREATMENT

Ongoing research continues to advance CF treatment, with promising developments in gene therapy, CFTR modulators, and other innovative therapies:

1. Gene Therapy

Gene therapy aims to correct the underlying genetic defect in CF by delivering a functional copy of the CFTR gene to affected cells.

2. Novel CFTR Modulators

New CFTR modulators are being developed to target a wider range of CFTR mutations and improve the efficacy of existing treatments.

Managing cystic fibrosis requires a comprehensive approach that includes medications, therapies, nutritional support, and multidisciplinary care. By understanding and implementing these treatment modalities, healthcare providers can significantly improve the quality of life and outcomes for patients with CF.

DISCUSSION QUESTIONS

- What are the benefits and limitations of current CFTR modulator therapies in treating cystic fibrosis?
- How can a multidisciplinary approach enhance the effectiveness of cystic fibrosis treatment plans?

MODULE THREE

LESSON ONE: RESPIRATORY CARE; BEST PRACTICES FOR RESPIRATORY THERAPISTS

Respiratory care is a cornerstone of cystic fibrosis (CF) management. Respiratory therapists play a critical role in providing care that helps patients maintain lung function, prevent infections, and manage symptoms. This lesson outlines the best practices for respiratory care in CF, offering detailed guidance on techniques, treatments, and patient education.

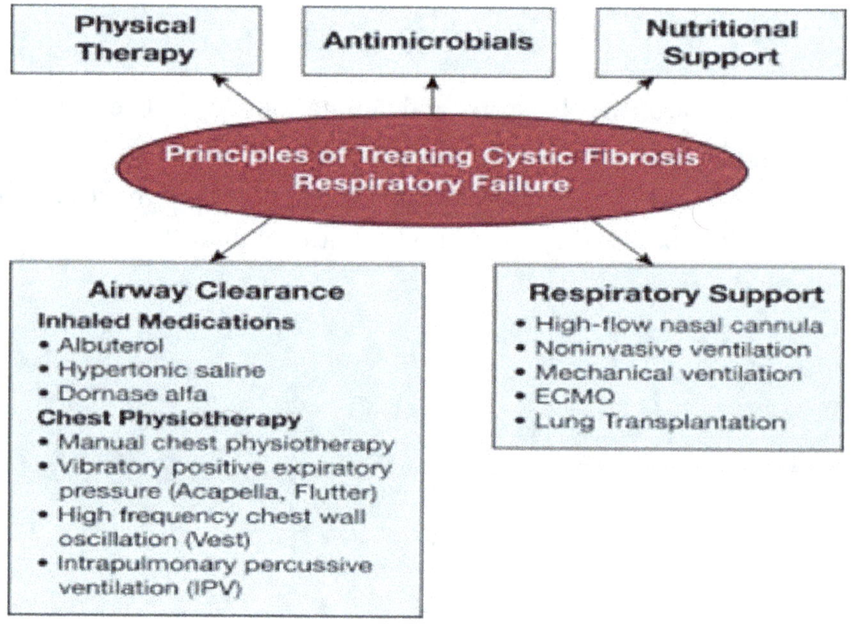

AIRWAY CLEARANCE TECHNIQUES (ACTS)

Effective airway clearance is essential for removing thick, sticky mucus from the lungs and preventing infections. Respiratory therapists should be well-versed in various ACTs and tailor these techniques to each patient's needs.

Chest Physiotherapy (CPT)

- Manual CPT: Involves percussion and vibration of the chest to loosen mucus, followed by coughing or huffing to expel it.
- Active Cycle of Breathing Techniques (ACBT): Combines breathing exercises, including deep breathing, huffing, and coughing, to mobilize and clear mucus.

Positive Expiratory Pressure (PEP) Therapy

- PEP Devices: These devices create resistance during exhalation, helping keep the airways open and move mucus towards the larger airways for clearance.
- Oscillating PEP (OPEP): Combines PEP therapy with oscillations to further loosen mucus.

High-Frequency Chest Wall Oscillation (HFCWO)

HFCWO Vest: A vest that delivers high-frequency vibrations to the chest, helping to loosen and mobilize mucus for easier clearance.

Autogenic Drainage

Self-Drainage Technique: Involves controlled breathing at different lung volumes to move mucus from smaller to larger airways without coughing.

INHALED MEDICATIONS

Inhaled medications are a cornerstone of CF respiratory care, providing direct delivery of drugs to the lungs.

Bronchodilators

- Short-Acting Beta-Agonists (SABAs): Albuterol and levalbuterol provide quick relief of bronchoconstriction and are often used before ACTs.

- Long-Acting Beta-Agonists (LABAs): Salmeterol and formoterol are used for maintenance therapy to control symptoms.

Mucolytics

- Dornase Alfa (Pulmozyme): An enzyme that breaks down DNA in mucus, reducing its viscosity. It is administered via nebulization.
- Hypertonic Saline: Inhaled hypertonic saline solution draws water into the airways, thinning the mucus and facilitating its clearance.

Antibiotics

Inhaled Antibiotics: Tobramycin and aztreonam target Pseudomonas aeruginosa, a frequent cause of lung infections in CF patients.

OXYGEN THERAPY

Oxygen therapy may be required for CF patients with advanced lung disease who experience low blood oxygen levels.

Indications for Oxygen Therapy

- Hypoxemia: Low blood oxygen levels, typically measured by pulse oximetry or arterial blood gas (ABG) analysis.
- Exacerbations: During acute exacerbations, supplemental oxygen may be needed to maintain adequate oxygenation.

Administration of Oxygen Therapy

- Nasal Cannula: Provides low-flow oxygen, suitable for mild hypoxemia.
- Non-Rebreather Mask: Delivers high concentrations of oxygen for more severe hypoxemia.
- Mechanical Ventilation: In severe cases, non-invasive or invasive mechanical ventilation may be required.

MANAGEMENT OF EXACERBATIONS

CF patients frequently experience exacerbations characterized by increased cough, sputum production, and respiratory symptoms.

Recognizing Exacerbations

- Increased Symptoms: Worsening cough, sputum production, and breathlessness.
- Fever: Often indicative of an underlying infection.
- Decreased Lung Function: Measured by spirometry, typically showing a decline in FEV1.

Treatment of Exacerbations

- Antibiotics: Oral, inhaled, or intravenous antibiotics to treat bacterial infections.
- Increased ACTs: More frequent airway clearance sessions to manage increased mucus production.
- Adjunct Therapies: Corticosteroids and bronchodilators to reduce inflammation and improve airflow.

PATIENT AND FAMILY EDUCATION

Educating patients and their families about CF and its management is crucial for ensuring adherence to treatment regimens and optimizing outcomes.

Teaching Airway Clearance Techniques

- Demonstration and Practice: Show patients and caregivers how to perform ACTs correctly and provide opportunities for hands-on practice.
- Individualized Plans: Tailor ACTs to each patient's needs and preferences, ensuring they are feasible and sustainable.

Medication Management

- Inhaler Techniques: Ensure patients use proper techniques for inhalers and nebulizers to maximize drug delivery.
- Adherence: Emphasize the importance of adhering to prescribed medication regimens and address any barriers to adherence.

Lifestyle and Wellness

- Exercise: Encourage regular physical activity, which can help improve lung function and overall health.
- Nutrition: Provide guidance on maintaining a high-calorie, high-protein diet to support growth and energy needs.

Multidisciplinary Collaboration

Effective respiratory care for CF requires collaboration among a multidisciplinary team, including pulmonologists, dietitians, nurses, and social workers.

Coordination of Care

- Regular Meetings: Hold regular team meetings to discuss patient progress, challenges, and treatment plans.
- Communication: Maintain open lines of communication with patients, families, and other healthcare providers to ensure cohesive care.

Advances in Respiratory Care

Ongoing research and technological advancements continue to improve respiratory care for CF patients.

Novel Therapies

- CFTR Modulators: New medications targeting specific CFTR mutations are expanding treatment options and improving outcomes.
- Gene Therapy: Promising developments in gene therapy aim to correct the underlying genetic defect in CF.

Respiratory therapists play a vital role in the care of CF patients, providing essential treatments and education to manage respiratory symptoms and improve quality of life. By following best practices and staying informed about advances in care, respiratory therapists can make a significant impact on the health and well-being of individuals with CF.

DISCUSSION QUESTIONS

- How can respiratory therapists tailor airway clearance techniques to meet the specific needs of individual cystic fibrosis patients?
- What are the latest advancements in respiratory care that have shown promise in improving outcomes for cystic fibrosis patients?

LESSON TWO: NUTRITIONAL MANAGEMENT AND SUPPORT: ESSENTIAL GUIDELINES FOR DIETITIANS

Nutritional management is a critical aspect of care for patients with cystic fibrosis (CF), as malnutrition and nutrient deficiencies can significantly impact overall health and disease progression. This lesson provides essential guidelines for dietitians on nutritional management and support for CF patients, focusing on optimizing growth, maintaining a healthy weight, and addressing specific nutrient needs.

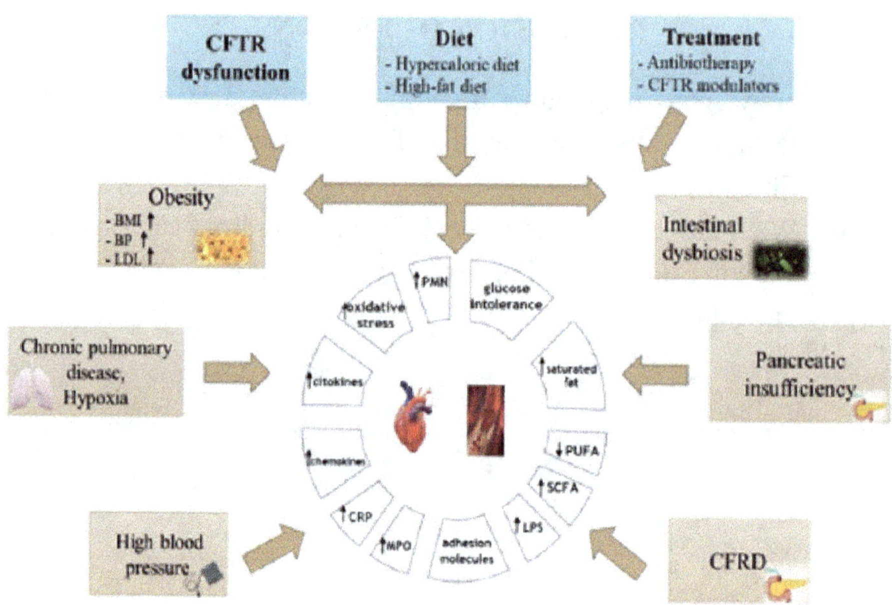

NUTRITIONAL CHALLENGES IN CF

Patients with CF face several nutritional challenges due to the disease's impact on the digestive system:

Pancreatic Insufficiency

- Malabsorption: The thick mucus in CF can block the release of digestive enzymes from the pancreas, leading to malabsorption of fats, proteins, and fat-soluble vitamins (A, D, E, and K).
- Nutrient Deficiencies: Malabsorption can result in deficiencies in essential nutrients, impacting growth, immune function, and overall health.

Increased Energy Needs

- Chronic Illness: The energy demands of chronic respiratory infections and inflammation increase overall energy requirements.
- Work of Breathing: Increased work of breathing due to lung disease further raises caloric needs.

Gastrointestinal Complications

- Gastroesophageal Reflux Disease (GERD): Common in CF patients and can exacerbate respiratory symptoms.
- Constipation and Distal Intestinal Obstruction Syndrome (DIOS): Thickened intestinal mucus can lead to blockages and bowel issues.

NUTRITIONAL ASSESSMENT

Regular nutritional assessments are essential to monitor growth, weight, and overall nutritional status:

Growth and Weight Monitoring

- Anthropometric Measurements: Regularly measure height, weight, and body mass index (BMI) to track growth and identify any deviations from expected patterns.
- Growth Charts: Use CF-specific growth charts to assess growth patterns and compare them with the general population.

Dietary Intake Evaluation

- 24-Hour Recall: Collect detailed information about the patient's dietary intake over the past 24 hours to assess nutrient intake and identify any gaps.
- Food Frequency Questionnaires: Use these questionnaires to evaluate habitual dietary intake and ensure a balanced and adequate diet.

Laboratory Assessments

- Nutrient Levels: Regularly measure blood levels of fat-soluble vitamins, essential minerals, and other critical nutrients to detect deficiencies early.
- Pancreatic Function Tests: Assess pancreatic function through stool tests for fecal elastase and other markers of malabsorption.

NUTRITIONAL INTERVENTIONS

Dietitians play a crucial role in developing and implementing nutritional interventions to address the unique needs of CF patients:

High-Calorie, High-Protein Diet

- Caloric Intake: Aim for caloric intake levels 1.5 to 2 times higher than the general population to meet increased energy demands.
- Protein Intake: Ensure adequate protein intake to support growth, muscle maintenance, and immune function.

Pancreatic Enzyme Replacement Therapy (PERT)

- Enzyme Supplementation: Prescribe pancreatic enzyme supplements with all meals and snacks to aid in the digestion and absorption of nutrients.

- Dosage Adjustment: Adjust enzyme dosages based on dietary fat content and symptoms of malabsorption, such as steatorrhea (fatty stools) and abdominal pain.

Vitamin and Mineral Supplementation

- Fat-Soluble Vitamins: Provide supplements of vitamins A, D, E, and K to prevent deficiencies and support overall health.
- Other Nutrients: Ensure adequate intake of calcium, iron, zinc, and other essential minerals to support growth and immune function.

Management of Gastrointestinal Complications

- GERD: Recommend dietary modifications, such as smaller, more frequent meals and avoiding trigger foods, along with medications as needed.
- Constipation and DIOS: Encourage adequate hydration, fiber intake, and the use of stool softeners or laxatives as needed to prevent blockages.

FEEDING STRATEGIES

Effective feeding strategies can help ensure adequate nutritional intake and address any feeding challenges:

Infant Feeding

- Breastfeeding and Formula: Support breastfeeding whenever possible and provide high-calorie formulas to meet increased energy needs.
- Complementary Feeding: Introduce nutrient-dense complementary foods around six months of age, focusing on high-calorie, high-protein options.

Child and Adolescent Feeding

- Frequent Meals and Snacks: Encourage multiple small meals and snacks throughout the day to increase caloric intake.

- Meal Planning: Work with families to plan balanced, nutrient-dense meals that are appealing and easy to prepare.

Adult Feeding

- Tailored Diet Plans: Develop individualized diet plans that consider the patient's lifestyle, preferences, and any comorbidities.
- Nutritional Counseling: Provide ongoing counseling and support to address any dietary challenges and ensure adherence to nutritional recommendations.

NUTRITIONAL EDUCATION AND SUPPORT

Educating patients and their families about nutritional management is vital for long-term success:

Patient and Family Education

- Nutritional Needs: Explain the increased energy and nutrient needs associated with CF and the importance of adhering to dietary recommendations.
- Enzyme Use: Educate patients and caregivers on the proper use of pancreatic enzyme supplements, including timing and dosage adjustments.

Multidisciplinary Collaboration

- CF Care Team: Work closely with the CF care team, including pulmonologists, gastroenterologists, nurses, and social workers, to provide comprehensive care.
- Regular Follow-Ups: Schedule regular follow-up appointments to monitor nutritional status, adjust interventions, and provide ongoing support.

ADVANCES IN NUTRITIONAL MANAGEMENT

Ongoing research and advancements in CF care continue to improve nutritional management strategies:

Nutritional Supplements

- New Formulations: Development of new formulations of pancreatic enzyme supplements and nutritional supplements tailored to CF patients' needs.
- Probiotics and Prebiotics: Emerging research on the potential benefits of probiotics and prebiotics in improving gut health and nutrient absorption.

Nutritional management is a critical component of care for patients with cystic fibrosis. By following these essential guidelines and collaborating with the multidisciplinary care team, dietitians can significantly improve the nutritional status, growth, and overall health of individuals with CF.

DISCUSSION QUESTIONS

- How do nutritional needs change throughout the lifespan of a cystic fibrosis patient, and what are the key considerations for dietitians?
- What strategies can dietitians use to address the common gastrointestinal complications associated with cystic fibrosis?

MODULE FOUR

LESSON ONE: PSYCHOLOGICAL AND SOCIAL CONSIDERATIONS IN CF CARE

Cystic fibrosis (CF) is a chronic, life-limiting condition that significantly impacts patients' psychological and social well-being. This lesson addresses the psychological and social considerations in CF care, providing healthcare providers with insights and strategies to support patients and their families effectively.

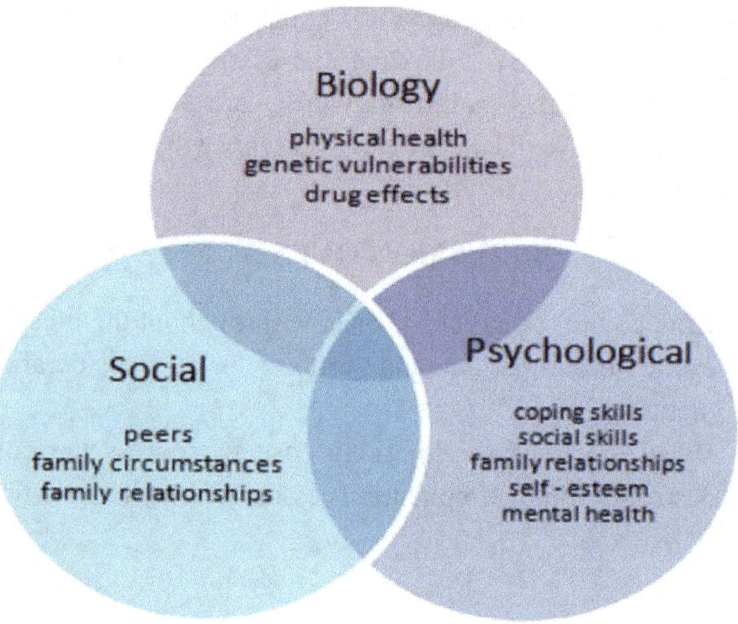

PSYCHOLOGICAL IMPACT OF CF

CF affects patients' mental health in various ways, from the stress of daily management to the emotional toll of living with a chronic illness:

Anxiety and Depression

- Prevalence: Anxiety and depression are common among CF patients due to the burden of disease management and uncertainty about the future.
- Screening: Regularly screen for anxiety and depression using validated tools such as the Hospital Anxiety and Depression Scale (HADS) or the Patient Health Questionnaire (PHQ-9).

Coping with Chronic Illness

- Emotional Resilience: Support the development of emotional resilience through counseling, support groups, and coping strategies.
- Therapeutic Interventions: Cognitive-behavioral therapy (CBT) and other therapeutic approaches can help patients manage stress and emotional challenges.

SOCIAL IMPACT OF CF

The social impact of CF includes the effects on relationships, education, and employment:

Family Dynamics

- Caregiver Burden: The demands of managing CF can lead to caregiver burnout and stress. Provide support and resources for caregivers to help them cope.
- Sibling Impact: Siblings of CF patients may experience feelings of neglect or jealousy. Encourage open communication and provide support for siblings.

Education and Employment

- School Support: Work with schools to ensure that CF patients receive the accommodations they need to succeed academically, such as flexible attendance policies and individualized education plans (IEPs).

- Workplace Accommodations: Assist adult patients in navigating workplace challenges and securing necessary accommodations to manage their health.

SOCIAL SUPPORT NETWORKS

Strong social support networks are crucial for the well-being of CF patients and their families:

Peer Support

- Support Groups: Encourage participation in CF support groups, where patients and families can share experiences, offer mutual support, and reduce feelings of isolation.
- Online Communities: Online forums and social media groups can provide additional support and resources for patients and caregivers.

Community Resources

- Financial Assistance: Connect patients and families with community resources for financial assistance, including grants, insurance support, and charitable organizations.
- Respite Care: Provide information on respite care services to give caregivers a break and reduce stress.

PALLIATIVE CARE AND END-OF-LIFE PLANNING

Palliative care focuses on improving the quality of life for CF patients by addressing physical, emotional, and spiritual needs:

Palliative Care Services

- Symptom Management: Provide comprehensive symptom management, including pain relief, respiratory support, and nutritional counseling.
- Psychosocial Support: Offer counseling and support for patients and families to address emotional and spiritual concerns.

Advance Care Planning

- End-of-Life Discussions: Engage in open and compassionate conversations about end-of-life preferences and advance care planning.
- Documentation: Ensure that patients' wishes are documented in advance directives and that all members of the care team are aware of these preferences.

INTEGRATING PSYCHOLOGICAL AND SOCIAL CARE INTO CF MANAGEMENT

A holistic approach to CF care involves integrating psychological and social support into the overall management plan:

Multidisciplinary Collaboration

- CF Care Team: Include psychologists, social workers, and other mental health professionals as part of the CF care team to address the psychological and social needs of patients.
- Regular Assessments: Conduct regular assessments of patients' psychological and social well-being as part of routine CF care.

Patient and Family Education

- Mental Health Awareness: Educate patients and families about the importance of mental health and the impact of CF on emotional well-being.
- Resource Availability: Provide information about available mental health resources and encourage their use as needed.

Addressing the psychological and social aspects of cystic fibrosis is essential for comprehensive care. By recognizing and supporting the mental health and social needs of CF patients and their families, healthcare providers can help improve their quality of life and overall well-being.

- How can healthcare providers support the mental health and emotional well-being of cystic fibrosis patients and their families?
- What are the unique challenges faced by adolescents with cystic fibrosis during the transition to adult care, and how can they be mitigated?

MODULE FIVE

LESSON ONE: ADVANCES IN CYSTIC FIBROSIS RESEARCH AND FUTURE DIRECTIONS

The landscape of cystic fibrosis (CF) care is continually evolving, with ongoing research leading to significant advancements in understanding and treating the disease. This lesson explores the latest advances in CF research and potential future directions that promise to transform the lives of patients with CF.

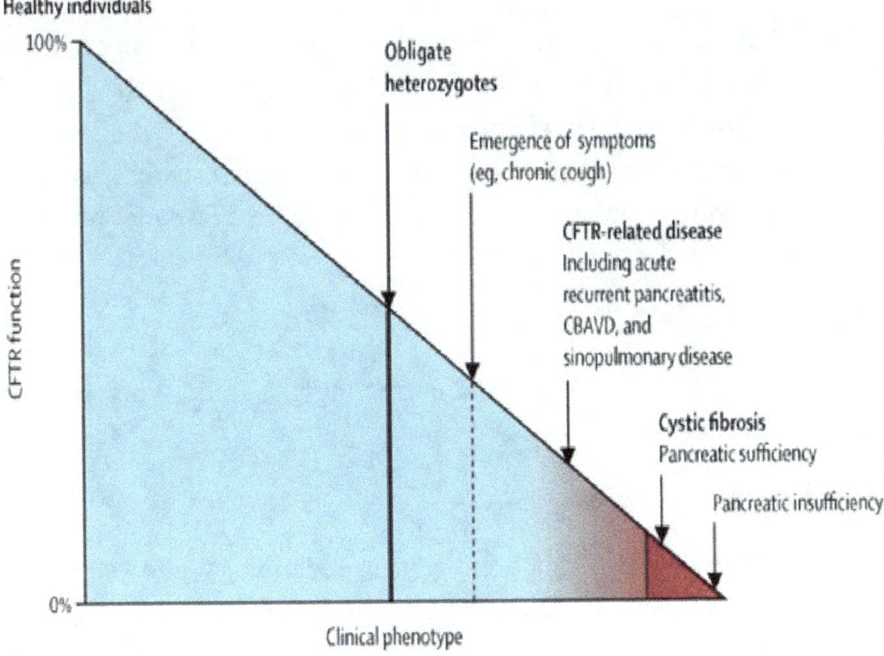

ADVANCES IN CFTR MODULATOR THERAPY

CFTR modulators have revolutionized CF treatment by targeting the underlying cause of the disease:

CFTR Modulator Classes

- Potentiators: Ivacaftor (Kalydeco) enhances the function of CFTR proteins at the cell surface, improving chloride transport.
- Correctors: Lumacaftor, tezacaftor, and elexacaftor help CFTR proteins fold correctly and reach the cell surface.
- Combination Therapies: Triple-combination therapies, such as elexacaftor/tezacaftor/ivacaftor (Trikafta), target multiple aspects of CFTR protein function, providing benefits to a broader range of CF mutations.

Expanding Eligibility

- Genetic Screening: Advances in genetic screening enable precise identification of CF mutations, allowing for tailored treatment with CFTR modulators.
- Research on Rare Mutations: Ongoing research aims to develop modulators effective for rare CFTR mutations that currently lack targeted treatments.

GENE THERAPY

Gene therapy holds promise for correcting the underlying genetic defect in CF:

Gene Editing Techniques

- CRISPR-Cas9: This gene-editing technology allows precise modifications of the CFTR gene to correct mutations directly.
- Viral Vectors: Delivery of functional CFTR genes to airway cells using viral vectors shows potential for long-term correction of CFTR defects.

Challenges and Progress

- Delivery Methods: Improving the efficiency and safety of gene delivery to target cells remains a key challenge.

- Clinical Trials: Early-phase clinical trials are underway to evaluate the safety and efficacy of gene therapy approaches for CF.

NOVEL THERAPEUTICS AND APPROACHES

Research continues to explore new therapeutic avenues beyond CFTR modulators and gene therapy:

Anti-Inflammatory Agents

- Targeting Inflammation: Novel anti-inflammatory agents aim to reduce chronic lung inflammation and slow disease progression.
- Immune Modulation: Modulating the immune response to prevent excessive inflammation and tissue damage is a promising area of research.

Mucus Modulation

- Mucolytics: New mucolytic agents aim to reduce mucus viscosity and improve clearance from the airways.
- Hydration Therapies: Therapies that enhance airway hydration and mucus clearance are under investigation.

ADVANCES IN DIAGNOSTICS

Improved diagnostic techniques are enhancing early detection and monitoring of CF:

Newborn Screening

- Early Detection: Advances in newborn screening allow for earlier diagnosis and initiation of treatment, improving outcomes.
- Biomarkers: Identifying novel biomarkers for early detection and monitoring disease progression is a focus of ongoing research.

Imaging Techniques

- Lung Imaging: Advanced imaging techniques, such as magnetic resonance imaging (MRI) and computed tomography (CT), provide detailed insights into lung structure and function.
- Non-Invasive Monitoring: Developing non-invasive methods to monitor lung health and treatment response is a priority.

PERSONALIZED MEDICINE

Personalized medicine aims to tailor treatment to individual patients based on their genetic makeup and disease characteristics:

Pharmacogenomics

- Drug Response: Understanding genetic factors that influence drug response helps optimize treatment regimens and minimize side effects.
- Precision Therapies: Personalized approaches consider patients' genetic profiles to select the most effective therapies.

Patient-Specific Models

- Organoids and Cell Models: Developing patient-specific organoids and cell models enables testing of personalized treatments in a laboratory setting.
- Data Integration: Integrating genetic, clinical, and environmental data helps refine personalized treatment strategies.

FUTURE DIRECTIONS AND INNOVATIONS

The future of CF research holds exciting possibilities for further advancements in treatment and care:

Stem Cell Therapy

- Regenerative Medicine: Stem cell therapy aims to replace damaged cells and tissues with healthy ones, offering potential for long-term correction of CF defects.
- Research Progress: Ongoing research explores the potential of stem cells to repair and regenerate lung tissue in CF patients.

Artificial Intelligence (AI) and Machine Learning

- Predictive Analytics: AI and machine learning can analyze large datasets to predict disease progression and treatment response.
- Clinical Decision Support: AI-driven tools assist healthcare providers in making informed treatment decisions based on individual patient data.

The advances in cystic fibrosis research and emerging therapies offer hope for improving the lives of CF patients. By staying informed about the latest developments and integrating innovative approaches into clinical practice, healthcare providers can continue to enhance care and outcomes for individuals with CF.

DISCUSSION QUESTIONS

- How have recent advancements in CFTR modulator therapies changed the landscape of cystic fibrosis treatment?
- What potential do gene therapy and stem cell therapy hold for the future of cystic fibrosis care, and what challenges must be overcome to realize their full potential?

MODULE SIX

LESSON ONE: CASE STUDIES AND PRACTICAL APPLICATIONS

This lesson presents case studies that illustrate practical applications of the principles and treatments discussed in previous lessons. These case studies highlight the complexities of managing cystic fibrosis (CF) and demonstrate the importance of a comprehensive, multidisciplinary approach to care.

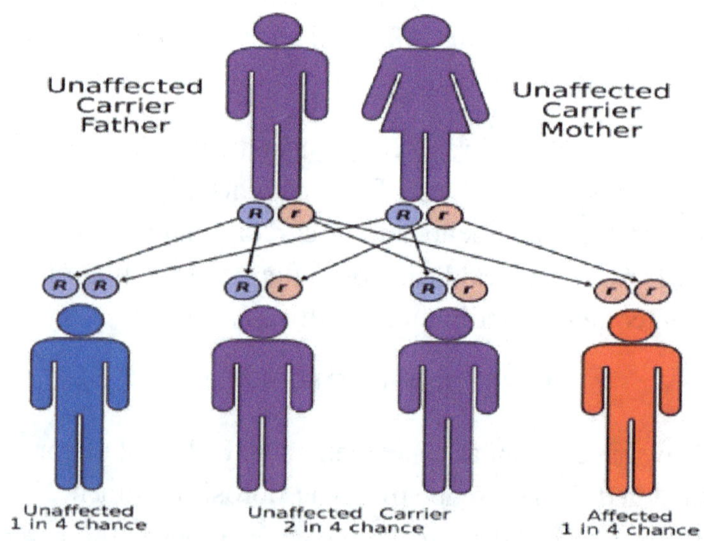

CASE STUDY 1: EARLY DIAGNOSIS AND INTERVENTION

Patient Profile:

- Name: Emily
- Age: 2 months
- Diagnosis: CF diagnosed through newborn screening

Clinical Presentation:

- Symptoms: Failure to thrive, frequent respiratory infections, and fatty stools
- Family History: No known family history of CF

INTERVENTIONS AND OUTCOMES:

Nutritional Support:

- Pancreatic Enzyme Replacement Therapy (PERT): Initiated to manage malabsorption and improve nutrient intake.
- High-Calorie Formula: Provided to support growth and weight gain.

Airway Clearance Techniques (ACTs):

- Chest Physiotherapy (CPT): Parents were trained in CPT techniques to help clear mucus from Emily's lungs.
- Inhaled Medications: Initiated dornase alfa to reduce mucus viscosity and improve clearance.

Multidisciplinary Care:

- CF Care Team: Regular follow-ups with a multidisciplinary team, including a pulmonologist, dietitian, and respiratory therapist.
- Family Education: Comprehensive education provided to Emily's parents about CF management and the importance of adherence to treatments.

Outcome:

- Growth and Development: Significant improvement in growth parameters and overall health.
- Symptom Management: Reduction in respiratory infections and improved digestion and nutrient absorption.

CASE STUDY 2: ADOLESCENT TRANSITION TO ADULT CARE

Patient Profile:

- Name: Jake
- Age: 17 years
- Diagnosis: CF diagnosed at birth

Clinical Presentation:

- Symptoms: Chronic cough, frequent pulmonary exacerbations, and declining lung function.
- Complications: CF-related diabetes (CFRD) diagnosed at age 15.

INTERVENTIONS AND OUTCOMES:

Respiratory Management:

- CFTR Modulator Therapy: Initiated elexacaftor/tezacaftor/ivacaftor (Trikafta) to target Jake's specific CFTR mutation and improve lung function.
- Airway Clearance Techniques (ACTs): Enhanced ACT regimen, including high-frequency chest wall oscillation (HFCWO) and inhaled hypertonic saline.

Diabetes Management:

- Insulin Therapy: Adjusted insulin regimen to manage blood glucose levels effectively.
- Nutritional Counseling: Provided dietary guidance to balance CF nutritional needs and diabetes management.

Transition Planning:

- Transition Program: Enrolled in a CF transition program to prepare for the move to adult CF care.

- Education and Support: Provided education about adult CF care and resources to support the transition.

Outcome:

- Lung Function: Stabilization and improvement in lung function with reduced frequency of exacerbations.
- Diabetes Control: Better management of CFRD with improved blood glucose levels.
- Successful Transition: Smooth transition to adult CF care with ongoing support and monitoring.

CASE STUDY 3: MANAGING ADVANCED CF AND LUNG TRANSPLANTATION

Patient Profile:

- Name: Sarah
- Age: 32 years
- Diagnosis: CF diagnosed at age 6 months

Clinical Presentation:

- Symptoms: Severe lung disease with frequent exacerbations, oxygen dependency, and declining quality of life.
- Complications: Advanced liver disease and malnutrition.

INTERVENTIONS AND OUTCOMES:

Pre-Transplant Management:

- Comprehensive Assessment: Evaluated by a multidisciplinary team for lung transplantation eligibility.
- Nutritional Support: Intensive nutritional interventions, including enteral feeding, to improve nutritional status pre-transplant.

Lung Transplantation:

- Surgery: Underwent successful bilateral lung transplantation.
- Post-Transplant Care: Intensive post-transplant care, including immunosuppressive therapy and monitoring for complications.

Rehabilitation and Recovery:

- Pulmonary Rehabilitation: Enrolled in a pulmonary rehabilitation program to regain strength and lung function post-transplant.
- Ongoing Monitoring: Regular follow-ups with the transplant team to monitor lung function and overall health.

Outcome:

- Improved Quality of Life: Significant improvement in respiratory function and overall quality of life.
- Reduced Hospitalizations: Decrease in hospitalizations and pulmonary exacerbations post-transplant.
- Continued Multidisciplinary Care: Ongoing multidisciplinary care to manage long-term health and prevent complications.

These case studies highlight the importance of personalized, multidisciplinary care in managing cystic fibrosis. By applying the principles and treatments discussed in this guide, healthcare providers can optimize outcomes and improve the quality of life for individuals with CF.

DISCUSSION QUESTIONS

- How can healthcare providers use case studies to improve clinical practice and patient outcomes in cystic fibrosis care?
- What lessons can be learned from the successful management of complex cystic fibrosis cases that can be applied to general patient care?

CONCLUSION

Cystic fibrosis (CF) is a complex and multifaceted disease that presents significant challenges for patients, families, and healthcare providers. This comprehensive guide underscores the importance of a multidisciplinary approach to CF care, incorporating the latest advancements in diagnosis, treatment, and supportive care to optimize patient outcomes. Healthcare providers, including doctors, nurses, respiratory therapists, dietitians, psychologists, and social workers, must work collaboratively to deliver comprehensive and compassionate care. Education and ongoing training are essential for staying informed about the latest advancements and best practices in CF care.

Empowering patients and their families with knowledge and resources enables them to take an active role in managing the disease. Supportive care, education on treatment adherence, and access to community resources contribute to better health outcomes and improved quality of life. As research progresses and new treatments emerge, the outlook for individuals with cystic fibrosis continues to improve. By embracing a multidisciplinary approach and fostering a collaborative care environment, healthcare providers can make significant strides in enhancing the lives of those affected by CF.

Cystic fibrosis healthcare education is a dynamic and evolving field that demands a comprehensive, informed, and patient-centered approach. Through dedication, innovation, and compassion, we can continue to advance the standards of care and offer hope to those living with this challenging disease.

REFERENCES

- Bell, S.C., De Boeck, K., & Amaral, M.D. (2020). *New pharmacological approaches for cystic fibrosis: What does the future hold? Expert Opinion on Pharmacotherapy.*
- Castellani, C., Assael, B.M., & Cipolli, M. (2018*). Cystic fibrosis: Early diagnosis and treatment. Current Opinion in Pediatrics.*
- Cutting, G.R. (2015). *Cystic fibrosis genetics: From molecular understanding to clinical application. Nature Reviews Genetics.*
- Davis, P.B., Drumm, M., & Konstan, M.W. (2016). *Cystic fibrosis. American Journal of Respiratory and Critical Care Medicine.*
- Farrell, P.M. (2018). *The prevalence of cystic fibrosis in the European Union. Journal of Cystic Fibrosis.*
- Flume, P.A., VanDevanter, D.R., & Fletcher, J.G. (2020). *Strategies for optimizing cystic fibrosis care in the 21st century. Chest.*
- Mall, M.A., & Hartl, D. (2020). *CFTR: cystic fibrosis and beyond. European Respiratory Journal.*
- Ratjen, F., & Bell, S.C. (2019). *Cystic fibrosis: Modern management and prognosis. Respiratory Medicine.*
- Riordan, J.R. (2008). *CFTR function and prospects for therapy. Annual Review of Biochemistry.*
- Rowe, S.M., Miller, S., & Sorscher, E.J. (2005). *Cystic fibrosis. New England Journal of Medicine.*